Land Without Maps

The Camden Poetry Group Anthology 2012

Edited by:
Judeth Miller
Pauline Drayson

Cover image by David Miller

Published 2012
by Lilyville Press

© The Camden Poetry Group
Published 2012

ISBN 987-0-9560207-3-4

Printed in Great Britain by
QP Printing
07593 025 013

Preface:

At the point of naming this the 14th Anthology of the Camden Poetry Group, and having read and re-read the poems, we reached an impasse. How do you choose a title and thus label such a diverse collection of work, so different in subject matter, style and length? We were on the verge of settling for a phrase that was safe but lacklustre, when my co-editor Pauline Drayson brought to the last meeting before the long summer break, a new poem, the title of which resonated with all present.

Poetry is indeed a Land Without Maps – we all follow different uncharted routes, different emotional and spiritual journeys and use different styles to reach the final expression of our poetic thought. The readers too, bring their life experience and have their individual responses to our end results.

I would like to thank Pauline Drayson not only for the title, but for her support and decisive editorial skills; also thanks to Hannah Hobsbaum-Kelly for her continued support as previous chair of the Camden Poetry Group and senior editor of Lilyville Press.

The Camden Poetry Group has existed for 45 years and continues to evolve and attract new members of all ages who bring their different talents and life experience. We work within a spirit of solid, constructive criticism and friendly support.

It is therefore with great pleasure that I commend this anthology to you the reader, hoping that in this Land Without Maps, you will find some recognisable landmarks.

Judeth Miller

Editors:
Judeth Miller
Pauline Drayson

Editorial address:
16 Mylne Close,
Upper Mall,
London, W6 9TE
camdenpoetrygroup@live.co.uk

Publisher:
Lilyville Press,
64 Lilyville Road,
London SW6 5DW
lilyvillepress@live.co.uk

Acknowledgements:

Copyright remains the property of the individual poets or their intellectual heirs

Pauline Drayson's *Red October* was published in the Ham and High.

Hannah Kelly's *On Loan, The Pilgrimage* and *The Cross* were all published in Poetry Church magazine.

Rachel Silbert's *A Poem* was published in *Songs of Transformation* 1999. *Walking Softly* was published in *Walking Softly, Poems 2009-2010* pub 2011

Jane Smith's *Disclaimer, In Autumn* & *In Extramadura* were published in a privately produced *Collected Poems.*

Judeth Miller's *The Long Straight Road* was published on the RSC website as part of the Adelaide Road Project with Aoife Mannix.

Contents

Continued over

contents continued

Climbing Rose

Hold me with the walls of practicality,
'Spersed with the seeds of common sense,
Surround my dreams with sense and sensibility,
Here, now, this present tense.

'Spersed with seeds of common sense,
Give me the air I need to breathe,
Here, now, this present tense,
Spray my form against disease.

Give me the air I need to breathe,
Strengthen my leaves of self-defence,
Spray my form against disease,
Submerge me in an oceanic sense.

Strengthen my leaves of self-defence,
Sheltering flowers that grow pure and wild.
Submerge me in an oceanic sense.
You are the Mother, I am the child.

Sheltering flowers that grow pure and wild.
Deepen my roots into the earth,
I am the Mother, you are the child,
Climbing rose about to birthe.

Deepen my roots into the earth,
Surround my dreams with sense and sensibility,
Climbing rose about to birthe,
Hold me with the walls of practicality,

Aria Datta

So Gently

Quietly, and oh so gently, you appear beside me,
"Is this a butterfly?" you ask in a whisper.
A centimetre creature walks on thread-thin legs
Across your hand. You raise it level with my eyes
And I see how the emergent wings are stuck
Drying in the April sunshine.

I explain this moment of creation and your eyes
Enlarge with the wonder of it, I too hold out my hand
To provide a temporary platform and released
From responsibility, you exhale, and wings, pearly white
Spotted with delicate sage, achieve a hesitant, cautious flutter.
"Oh," you murmur, oh so gently.

The thread legs totter across our hands, trusting
Our closeness and accord. I explain this creature is
Growing like you, dependent before independence.
Together we examine and deconstruct this miracle
Until softly and oh so gently, the wings part company
And two divides into four, lifting in the breeze.

This small interaction has nearly passed. Though not
Yet four, you understand instinctively, how nurturing
Is a quiet and softly breathing time and we enjoy this
Daily miracle within its context, learning with sensitivity,
To see. The butterfly, suddenly confident, gracefully
And oh so gently, flies.

Judeth Miller

Winter Sky

This morning the sun shines
For half an hour
Transparent azure sky, white cloud –
dashed trails of aeroplanes, sky-wide.
The white sloping roof opposite,
picked out by the sun.
Birds various rest there; pause.

Grey clouds slowly thicken,
tumble in at the windows,
softly bulbous,
pile on pile.
Dusk at three-thirty, dark at four.

5 January 2011

Light thrusts upwards,
          sings as it thrusts –
Light containing light

7 January 2011

Anthea Bennett

A Poem

Pared down and terse
or richly ornamental,
a poem goes beyond
our daily dialogue,
focussing attention on
a hidden seam of thought –
a tiny holograph
taken from a poet's soul,
lying vulnerable
on the page, open
to random scrutiny.
Its magic draws us
to the unexpected joy
of heightened vision.

Rachel Silbert

Disclaimer

I've mentally lined my lovers up
And done a swift review.
Relax, relax, relax, relax -
This is not about you.
This is all about me, my heart,
My grief, my bliss, my pain.
Some of it I would not revisit.
Some I would do again.
It's all been fascinating.
I can't say less than that.
And the joy of this kind of retrospective
Is no-one knows where it's at.
Friends who have gone the course with me
Might make an informed guess,
But a poet's privilege is to lie,
So they won't have much success.
Oh, the plus side of a mis-spent life,
The reward of all those tears,
Is copy enough to keep me going
For years and years and years.

Jane Smith

Serendipity

Two young men sat either side of me
On my left a suit
He looked nice enough, solid, reliable
On my right a Greek God
We left the ground and soared to the heavens.

I breathed in the recycled air
Mixed with a dose of testosterone
We were gliding on clouds
My fantasies floated and focused
On the Adonis to my right,
Large hands splayed on his knees,
One hand tapping rhythmically.
I marvelled at the restlessness of youth
Forever in motion.
His head turned to the window
I could linger on his bleached zig-zag hair
Stopping just short of his shirt collar.
Evocative.

It was a short flight
Down we came
Down I came
We landed
I landed

I muttered something inconsequential to Adonis
He flashed me a warm smile.
Another hunk of testosterone handed me my suitcase.

I was not totally invisible
Just an aging woman, but only on the outside
Not all things can be hijacked by the passage of time.

Rywa Weinberg

Black Boots

In Northampton long ago you came to birth
In that dogged, slow, imperious way a blacksmith
Hammers out an iron hoof. So the Victorian shoemaker
Hammered down your heel, and deftly pared the trimmings
From your stitched and weltered sole. He squinted for
                                    the slightest flaw:
Held them up for proud inspection, then bagged,
                                    boxed, and sped them
Into the fray! Up steps- down cobbled passages-
                                    along horse shitten streets
Roads, entry-ways, stepping on, stepped on, squelched,
                                    battered and mauled:
Briskly brushed, blackened, dubbed, lick-spittled,
                                    good service for a squaddy
A bus-conductor or policeman, a gardener or a tramp.

Then, inexplicably you slipped out of service. Perhaps the
                                    gardener fell ill
Before he could destroy you with persistent digging?
                                    Perhaps the tramp died
In a ditch: you slyly stripped from him in the morgue,
                                    then quickly shoved
Into a cupboard, not cleared out until the morgue
                                    became a theatre,
When the wardrobe lady smilingly presented you
To a penurious local museum.

So here you are
As scrutinised by children or the elderly as long ago
A sergeant or inspector on parade. `Must `ave bin `eavy eh?
Must `ave bin awkward lacin' up'`I say, must have made
                                    policemen look like clowns-
What what!' Then I remember Van Gogh's boots, his straw-woven
                                    chair, remember
Fields, orchards, artists; and feel once more
The sterling make and measure of you through
My squinting orifice of years.

John Jarvis Hands

Strictly Come Clog Dancing goes to Forty Hells

Hobgoblins love to clog dance
they learn as little sprites
to strut their stuff
and stomp their feet
in little wooden shoes
until they're grown
and then they wear
their grown-up hobnailed
wooden clogs to practice
and compete, and once a year
in goblin time (more frequently
for us) their heats hot up
their finals boil and finally erupt
with drunken brawls and
and merriment and all night
celebrations, until they trash
themselves, the hall and
everything in sight.

Hobgoblins love to party
with all their freaky friends,
so viral flash mob messages
vibrate on gnarly gnome phones
and clad in grotesque party gear
they slip into my sleeping form
and rock their nightshade carnival.

Tonight's the Halloween parade
the otherworld is out in force:
vajazzled elves, the fallen kind,
in gilded threads of gossamer
seek lusty pierced dwarves with tats
they know will delve deep secret caves,
long and hard for hidden gems;

hoochie mama ghouls in pan stick,
boots and big hair gleaming fine
set their sights on horny gremlins,
to get inside their steaming systems;
limber sprites in skin tight lycra
with nymphs inspired by Lady Gaga,
weave and writhe their sexy way

to Morris dancing leprechauns
decked out in biker leather gear;
the bogies are moustached and macho
eyeing up the gorgeous gnomes,
and off the hook they surf the crowd
inciting demon twisticuffs.

I relish your diversity and if I had energy
like yours, I'd join you in your joyous gigs,
and gladly whirl the nights away.

I've opened Forty Hells Frumunda,
a funky cavern underground. Go there
from now on or elsewhere, join the
naiads and the undines, even angels for your fun:
my body elementals needs their body,
and so, I find, do I.

Lesley Hannah

Why....?

Looking at me so woefully,
you say:
Because fish have eyes

You are a Vegetarian,
The ones you see around,
Eating with a conscience
Growths in the ground.

Mushroom-stalked heads,
Potatoes cross-eyed,
Carrots sport tops
Whilst onions cried.

Standing tree barks,
Sweet potatoes ooze
Sticky caramel blood
And Broccoli bruise.

Biscuits like a dip
In the warm bronze waves of tea,
Doughnuts on your china plate
Squeaking comfortably.

Par-snips, ra-dishes
Caressing dark green leaves,
Painless, cruelty-free ….indeed?
Chewing on beliefs.

You are a Vegetarian,
The ones you see around,
Eating with a conscience
Growths in the ground.

Why?

Looking at me so woefully
You say:
Because Fish have Eyes.

But, Dear Friend,
"Tomatoes Scream…"

And so do I.

Aria Datta

Walking Softly

I walk softly, gently,
on the green spring lawn,
taking care not to crush
those insouciant daisies
also heralding the spring,

as are the lilac tree
and the giant laburnum,
grown taller than this building,
a measure of my years of residence.

I sit in my favourite nook
Under a lush canopy
Of assorted leaves,
Which lean and sway
To catch the breeze
As it cavorts among them.

It curls around my body,
Swirls along my arms and legs,
Refreshes bleary tired eyes,
Whips up slow-moving blood.

Now I am barefoot,
Feel the smoothness of the grass,
Smell new growth around me,
Free my captive winter feet.

This spring is late,
June instead of April,
But it has come at last
With its life-affirming blessings –

The blessings to enjoy
my annual new beginnings;
No personal searing judgements,
No self-blame and no regrets.

I walk softly, gently, barefoot,
Among my qualities, learn again
To take life as it comes.

Rachel Silbert

Whilst Unpacking

We arrived here,
My stuff and I,
collectively crumpled,
moth-eaten, subdued.

And we cannot quite believe
our luck. There is – space – here
and light, and my back hurts but
perhaps we can – *live* here.

Unfurling reveals Stuff:
I have too much sellotape
and an unacknowledged
addiction to collection to collecting recipes.

Things have changed since
I last opened these boxes and
old books on new shelves
is right but - strange.

As I pause for tea,
dust-covered and awash
with memories, I find seeds
and planting materials.

Leaving the mess,
With relief for a moment,
I plant chives, coriander,
And water new roots with hope.

Rachel Buchanan

`Perhaps one day I will heal'

First and last come love and the beloved –
jubilate, I love you, with exquisite joy –
your perception, your caring, your understanding.
The calm of your painting soothes comforts my soul

I dance slow quick quick slow.
I sing Halleluja with the hills.
The day dawns, splitting the darkness.
The cat stretches as he lies on my bed.

I am born again
into a new world.
My mother dies:
my father laughs: weeps laughs.

I am old with a lifetime behind me,
Holding Bach and Mahler, Eliot and Yeats.
Movements fragmented with joy and its glory,
Words evoking light and colour, and intense.

What of the future?
Is there a future? After birth comes death.
The calm of your painting soothes
Comforts my soul.

Anthea Bennett

On Loan

We are on loan to each other,
Friends as we are,
Ships that pass in the night,
Glad of the other's light,
Even in passing.

Lighthouses are static,
God's lighthouse
In each heart,
Even when the ships have crossed.

Hannah Kelly

Bill and Tommy

They lost their names to red
ink and dusty cabinets.

Loose lips sink ships! And
Other such requirements.

Behind the scenes in a
Shady basement of an

invisible mansion—
like bats in a belfry

a sound alive resonates
through silk-threaded webs

extending from there to here.
From their lofty position

above our heads float
numbers carrying

indecipherable names, lost
to red ink and dusty cabinets.

Felix Ortiz

The Falling Child

Do you see that child?
    He is falling.
His Feet are on the ground
But he is falling.
Oh yes, he is laughing,
Like every other child he jumps and climbs
But he is falling.

Once when the sky was blue, and he was small,
His parents sat so close.
Their two laps formed a swing – he nestled there,
Cradled, delirious, drinking in the lilt
Of their two voices; little sprays of sound
Fanned cool upon him; now
His mother faces east, his father west,
and in the waste between
                the child is falling.

Marjorie Wardle

A.S.

I look at this photograph of Alan,
stood before a pool of sunlight
which has bloomed over chequered fields
and the lower slopes of mountains;
a distant lake diffuses into mist:
he is a good artist
the pool could be of his own making

He stands securely, easily
upon a slope of loose scree,
giving access to his quiet thoughts:
he is dressed for walking over rough terrain,
through sudden changes in the shifting weather:
he is well shod
so as to mitigate the earth's intent;
his staff could be used to tender sheep

I remember the influence
a good man has on his surroundings
and I have no choice
but to come back to that foolishness
which is abandonment to God.

Roy Batt

Shocking

It was a shock –
He did not look like a beggar,
his clothes clean, uncrumpled.
He shattered my reverie
sitting beneath horse chestnuts.
"Give me 30p" he said.
I looked into the distance,
deaf to his voice, his request,
denying his very presence.
I gazed into the distance
wondering why "they always picked on me".

Not heeded, he turned away
Started walking up the hill,
Slowly working his way
Through a clutter of blank faces.

I relaxed my guard,
examined my own thoughts,
found I was holding 50p
in my hand, waiting for him
to walk down the hill towards me,
filled with remorse at not
responding in a kindlier way,
mollifying my conscience
by holding more than 30p
ready to offer him,
but setting a condition –
I'd give him the money
if he came back my way;
found I could not stir,
would not follow him up the hill
to fulfil his modest need.

What would I be like
Begging an indifferent world
For 30p to satisfy my hunger?
I dared not contemplate the thought,
turned my mind to other matters,
like the full bag of groceries
at my feet, and how expensive
each item had become.

Rachel Silbert

Lament for Camden Town and Kentish Town

These towns were your manor,
These grimy cobbled paths, leading to the dark canal.
The markets where you bought me flowers and wine,
And where you charmed the ladies in the fish shop,
Saw you most days.

When you were ill, I put your bets on for you in
                                 Mash's little shop
And when you won the pools (just once) you
                                    gave it all away.
You scorned the Heath, preferring pavements under your feet.

I wasn't the only one who loved you for your warm heart;
I was so lucky that you fancied me!
Now I love the places where you walked;
The pub where you played darts week after week,
The restaurants we liked (further up the hill).
I take the 24 bus you used to drive,
And gaze out of the window at the raffish,
tatty streets I formerly despised.

These streets are your place;
I wish with all my heart you were still here.

Jean Wallis

Songbirds

(For Billie ,Amy, Doris, Florence and Whitney)

The feathered dress is legendary.
For us, chromatic notes are pulled
On a conjurer's string from the throat.
We applaud those airy bones walking
The tightrope of melisma. Whether lark
helixing a honey yell or soft sting
of crow's world-knowing vinegar,
The thrill promises never to be gone.
We can smile as budgies multi-hue crew
Pass full rhyme lyrics, beak to beak,
Light on toy mirrors and flowered swings.
Then again, for us, the ache is temporary, sweet
When the nightingale reaches its peak
blood thick on a rose's stiletto.

When silence is falling
Some can go home, to the flow
Of clouds over branches, of summer rain
And some smash their frames against the ground
unchaining their echo, that hummable ghost.

Jane Sherberkov

The Pilgrimage

My life is one unceasing pilgrimage,
To find and keep the peace of Christ
Within these walls.

Daily, I make my spiritual journey,
Sometimes a coward,
Sometimes a hero.

The coward stopped by fear for Self,
The hero stepping forward
For fear of Self.

Between these two extremes,
I make my daily pilgrimage,
But always find His peace
Within these walls.

Hannah Kelly

The Horse and Cart

I never see him now, driving his horse and cart
By the side of the playing-field.

Sometimes in Ockley, on a Sunday
There is a gathering of gleaming coaches
And fine brushed steeds. He would be out of place
In such a setting –
His carriage is a box, his horse shabby and slow.

One day I was part of a cavalcade,
A line of traffic in the country lane
Beside the playing-field:
Ford Escorts, one Mercedes,
Assorted makes and colours jammed together,
Me and my bus in the rear.
No hooting, no impatience, just a slow
Measured procession; he was at its head,
Perched on his box, drawn by his pony,
Till he turned left, and the motorcade rolled on.

He was a god that day,
His steed flashing a golden mane,
The home-made box a carriage,
Cantering into the distance,
Whipped into unaccustomed speed
By scrolls of racing wind.

Marjorie Wardle.

The Long Straight Road

On the top of an ancient horse drawn fly,
I fly, seem to levitate, float above
the commonplace, glancing through windows to
the ordinary, gaudy and the grand.

Carrying a flask of lubricating joy
I fill my needs; a touch of spice, a scarf
of gossamer to hide my stranger-ness,
a hover mat to let the humps, the lumps
the bumps be unfelt by my aging bones.

This road is straight, long, not easy, I urge
to curve; when cast out, a Nash terrace brought
me tears; a bus swerve let me know London
was both nemesis and sweetest destiny.

So I follow my ancient Speed; parchment
map drawn in fine pen, colours bleached which once
vibrated from monk brewed, faith steeped inks.

It is autumn, low sun blinds the mundane
from my eyes. Russet colours, crumbly leaves
and the smell of trodden windfalls, cider
and spice rising from the wayside grass.
The blustering wind turns and become a
hurricane, shouting its force into trees
which creak and wail in anguished reply.
Then out of the urban wild, comes Sybil,
animatedly continuing a
conversation begun in nineteen seventy.

Journeys often seem to take me towards
the setting sun. I carry my babies'
clothes against my skin, inhale their love;
holding a capsule of forgetfulness
to erase the child I was, another,
an awakener to enhance the child
I have become – too late.

Here in the city, night falls, a slither
of salmon against navy blue, changing
hue as each second passes, until it
fades to deepest velvet indigo.

At peaceful destination a holy
place, scent of aged port; sacramental
drops of wine, portent of divine peace.

At long last, sleep and taste of hot lemons
souring in the mouth, breath soft spiced; and wrapped
around, the smell of clean wet hair.

Asleep I am alive to hope, still, but
still journeying; my straight road was a
perfect circle. I am returned to the
one I used to be – or maybe the me
I want to see, an oxymoron of
a life with this eternal voyaging.

Judeth Miller

Air

Elementals live within
the nooks and crannies of nature
often unseen
otherworldly
faeries, sprites, gnomes,
dryads and naiads.

Pan's pipes haunt me.
At Chalice Well I feel his presence
overshadow me,
The ancient yew is vibrant with life,
the red spring sings in tune
with the crocus studded grass.

I am in my element.

Lesley Hannah

Aspiration and Descent

To rise up further than others, to see in wide
Perspective, cities, cathedrals, towers,
To ferret out, to burrow where others seldom venture
In sea-caverns, vaults, even beneath mines and tunnels
Are surely challenges which might have been ignored.
But who is to reassure us? Who is to convince us our
Reckless enterprise should never be attempted?
When the sullen tide is in, should we desert, or linger near
The threatening shore?   There is no certainty,
No surety in nature: travel too near the edge and surely
Your opportunities for falling off are
Boundlessly increased? O unsorted, unfulfilled, unhappy
Questing one! A nature attuned, replete, is by nature
Seldom a happy one.

John Jarvis-Hands

Where Three Paths Meet

Here is a place, overlaid
When I am here, with things
That step out of time: a pair
Aslant the wooden park-seat
As they talk, then turn away:
They are gone again when I blink.

They come and go in a grey parade
Of couples, some of whom I knew,
All of whom lingered here,
Left together or parted.
Age, that makes them grey
To remembrance, took them
Together or drew them apart;
Whilst I, only remember my hurt.
And it is strange how there is
No blood to show
From a wounded heart
Which might bestrew
Such a place where lovers go.

It is a place where three
Paths meet, where some
Must have said `Your way or mine.'
Three paths must always mean choosing.

Only in summer I come
To hear the collared doves
And wood pigeons' duet
In the arbour of shade, so soothing,
Which winter makes dumb.
Mine is an ear of fancy
And yet, I muse it is what
They cannot forget that they murmur;
Some appeal in their soft word coo;
Louder, more urgent it sometimes seems
To bring lost hearts together again.
All down the years
They have called it,
And yet they have called it
All in vain.

Roger Taylor

Holy Thursday.

After the bells, the dancing candle light
The rising voices singing Gloria,
Feet are humbly, gently washed tonight
and kissed, in numinous act of love.

Then the final moment of despair
As wordless, hushed, the altar is stripped bare.

Hard and lonely is this night, living the hours
of lamentation, waiting as if no past time
had been, to draw upon, remember;
But knowing the prophesied betrayal.

It is raw and hard this night; internalised
Pain for which there is no soothing balm
but prayer, this holy silence in which to dare
to feel the empty depths of desolation.

In painful anticipation we too must share
Some shattered splinters of the wood of life
and death, Holy cross or Judas tree; His gift
Of choice for us and all humanity.

To go beyond this moment of despair
Are the painful hours of waiting, soul stripped bare.

Judeth Miller

The Cross

Triumphant, now,
That ploughman's
Wooden Cross,

So much despised,
And ridiculed -
It had a happy ending,

The pain cannot be forgotten,
Sometimes resuscitated,
But there is hope in Christ,

The bloodied
Crown of thorns,
A silver diadem.

Hannah Kelly

Apparitions

Somehow, somewhere, I shall see your face.
A moment may be all we are allowed,
Slipping between the bars of time and space.

You shape, then you dissolve. I give you chase.
The rain so heavy and the wind so loud.
Somehow, somewhere, I shall see your face.

Each time I glimpse you in a different place.
Often you turn aside, your head is bowed,
Slipping between the bars of time and space.

One day you disappeared without a trace.
I seemed to lose you in the Friday crowd.
Somehow, somewhere, I shall see your face.

The weeks go by, everything has its pace –
I see your shape etched in a cone of cloud,
Slipping between the bars of time and space.

Your tiny frame, its modesty and grace.
Hair in a knot, tied back, simple but proud.
Somehow, somewhere, I shall see your face,
Slipping between the bars of time and space.

Marjorie Wardle

Pushkin's Last and Longest Journey

Today
       was the first snow of the season and
Today
       we took our dear cat Pushkin to the animal crematorium.
Every tearful mile of the way (almost) we recalled how
he looked before he became too thin to survive: sleek and plump
with incisive, large owl-eyes. We remember how he sprang
over the fence like a fox or a deer when we called,
how he darted up the iron stairway to the kitchen, somehow
managing not to snag his paws in the interstices; how eagerly he
mooched around for food which he lately scarcely sniffed
before turning away from the choice fish we tenderly prepared
and eagerly proffered, like gifts to an indifferent African chief.
Pathetically he cried when doors inexplicably resisted
His enfeebled dabbing paws.

Today
       we took our ginger tabby Pushkin on his last and longest journey:
(he hated cars, and even more baskets, whether wire or wicker).
We talked to a large sympathetic equestrian lady, then handed over
A certain plump sum (for individual cremation plus ashes by return).
Then we lifted all that remained of our thin, wasted cat
On to an improvised altar lit by twenty pee candles.
We drove away hurriedly: hardly daring to snatch a backward look.
We left behind several years of our marriage and middle age, and
Some few snowflakes of guilt for having loved him so much.

John Jarvis Hands

In Remembrance

Walking this evening in summer's wood
I heard your name come softy
Through the light air
Like whispers in the wind.

The trembling waters of the lake
Seemed a voice calling out
The name I vowed to love forever.
And trees swaying in a harmony of green,
Restless at sunset evoked your presence.

I felt as if the whole of nature
Was calling, calling your name
            In remembrance.

P S Drayson

Love in a Letter

We might have had
children: they do not exist, though
in a sense they do

we had to ring-fence
our love, in case one of us
should violate it

our love keeps breaking
out afresh, as if it were
some happy illness

I watched the handling
of my letter to you, winced
at ineptitude

you talk about our love
for each other; tell me then
is it so much?

`Not expressible in
words,' you said: even so,
We are using them.

Roy Batt

Eighth of March

Umbrellas rise like wands and the rainfall falls
In this, our last appointment

We thread ourselves
through paths as familiar as our faults
while clouds toy like mediators and spread apart

Your smile resets thought
disputes resolve
or drift from context and discontinue

I see your breath
in the hollow platform
where trains curve and allocate shape

Stare past the exit sensation
of a full stop kissed square
on the forehead, the cheek

David Bann

The Sewing Class

On the third floor of a rickety building –
High enough to look the church clock in the face,
The green of the square misty through the windows,
Blurred, until the lamps appear in early evening
Premature, like over eager guests.

The sounds in the room gentle, absorbing
Whirr of the treadle machines, crackle of cotton,
Susurrus of silk,
Crunch of shears, soft thump of the iron.
Voices pitched low.
Even colours are muted here, cloth in apricot,
Lavender, blue; and the green of the square.
A place so female, so quiet.

My thought of you are never quiet –
Rising and falling down to awareness, ragged pain,
Up to surging life and dismay.
I feel I have fallen from this high building,
And every agonising movement of mind and body
Mixes with memories, and the shock of hitting
The ground.
Living on seems artificial, superfluous, a prolonged insincerity
Am I unworthy of love, of life?

The answer could be in your heart, your brain -
And in your wide set eyes.

Jean Wallis

Joanna's Birth Day, 8 June 1962

Out she slithered on Friday evening
In time for the Sabbath
Candles were lit in my head
She was blue tinged

After a slap
A cackle of sound exploded
And there she was
A living part of me, now separate
with slanting eyelids tightly closed

I wondered why the Chinese nurse
Looked fondly at her
She's not having my baby
I thought
And held her close

While looking furtively around
At the other mums
I sniffed her blood caked head
And was tempted to lick it clean
Instinctively, she began to suckle

We were connected again

Rywa Weinberg

The Needle of a Friday Night

It's as long as the world is tall and she
        smiles
then lets fly with the testing spurt

which separates splendidly like the
        unveiling
of the first fountain. But I've been here

too many times before, beside white
        walls,
on green, starch-folded linen beneath

god-light, through drunken slights and
        sleepless
nights — I've sleepwalked through

the walls of accident and emergency and
        sat
on eerie green plastic and metal next to

overworked coke can machines and
        end of night
train-wrecks, or simply the cold and

lonely and afraid in plaster cast with
        no ink-marks
and no story to tell of their own.

She misses the mark with the first stab
        in the dark
and I attempt a smile to let her know

'it's alright', but inside I'm fit to burst.
        Funny thing, pride.
I can't let her know that inside I'm a

child, but it's my adolescence that
        brought me
here tonight and it will probably see

me return — and maybe find me in some
        distant corner
of the world, waking me up for the 9.55

from King's Cross or the Gare du Nord to
        take me
speeding through Europe, then spit me

out on the floor of some coach at
        mid-day
half-way to the Horn of Africa — with

soiled streets and gung-ho police and
        cattle-drivers
and a thousand herded goats and
        real stars.

Felix Ortiz

The Best Things about Mondays

Your voice on the phone,
Languid and formal,
was a challenge, as
I could hear, somewhere,
a man beneath the job.

I worked hard,
in subsequent weeks,
to warm it up,
break it down,
make you laugh –

and I did! Your
incongruous chuckle
in our working
conversation,
My Prize, hard-won.

Should I go on,
in my success
to the next step?
To meet you, somehow,
it could be done;

or am I happy to leave it
at this, just this –
your voice in my ear,
as you laugh in your office
and I, smile alone, in mine.

Rachel Buchanan

Venetian Mastery

We know that you're a fake, a drifting city
Whose stones decay as vividly as leaves
In autumn, yet echo mean cacophonies
Of dirt, fool's good, rat-nibbled logs and thieves.
Some stockinged lens of love distorts our eyes:
The perspective of Renaissance galleries
Where Veronese rots. That bridge's sighs
Were tuned through torture forks but seas
Of kissing myths dissolve the despot's law –
We'll take the myth, take snaps of golden domes,
Say those who talk realpolitick are bores,
Blind to the artisan's blown glass foam.
Our flesh, shaken by white, flesh-eating waves
Hopes coffined art will salt, embalm, save.

Jane Sherberkov

Bacillus

Under sterile jars and decaying litmus
This great miracle of cells
Holds dimensions
Within our spotlight microscope

Some saturate their world
Shrivel to spores
And wait like spheres
For fractions or millions of years

Others continue their unique cascade
Repeating life
From invisible mass
Shifting existence like uncapped attention

February is the shortest month
But we didn't notice
We heard the fine complexity of rainfall
And rested our eyes outside.

David Bann

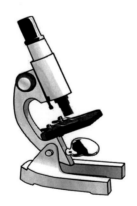

Friday 13th January 2012

Bright frosty day on Golders Hill
I photographed a leafless tree.
Portrait of a Dancing Tree, I thought,
my project for a class next week.

I stroked her creviced bark and thanked her,
Her trunk was warm to touch.
Yet basking in the self same sun,
the other trees were chilled.

I thought I saw her beating heart and seemed
to feel her pulsing sap. I called my friend to witness:
how curious this tree. And we became tree huggers
for a madcap sacred moment, then with

backs against the balmy bark we rested,
gloriously lifting up our faces to the light.
I saw a dryad smile delight and laughing all the while,
she mimicked human kisses on our sun touched skin.

Lesley Hannah

Spring Snow

Freezing toes pad
across the kitchen;
monet-curtains move:

snow flakes on....

my apple tree:
pale-lemon drops
precociously nibbled,
balancing blackbird;

upside down olive
flower tub, wind-swept,
a fez upon my soggy green;

white winter jasmine
adorned my wooden walls
many moons ago.

withered leaves reproach
from murky trenches,
stalking green spikes;

youthful leaves stretch
across the trellis.
whispering song;

pecking pigeons platter;
plumping, flathering wings
in a diangular rush over

the far right corner, where
my magnolia stands straight,
still, closed with
spring-buds,

as

the snow flakes on....

Aria Datta

Heat

This is a day for the fleshless,
Leave me white boned and dry
As a desert morsel
Or the chalk spiral of a sea shell stripped
On a sun stricken spit.

Grey heron flexed on an angle-poise pin
Scouts the witchery of water that sucks itself in
For shimmering succulence
- Dead bead eye evolves in one beat –
And stabs.

All ache transpires with relief.
And the hard bitten ghost
Skitters its gill husks
Over evaporate shingle.

Tessa Anslow

Beside

We carved our image
In the mountain

Against the burst terrain
Of a Canadian redwood

Two coins pressed
Against its porous outer skin
Then pushed inside

Each lap of life
        Sank and stretched above us

David Bann

In Autumn

The paddling pool, not more than two feet deep
At any point, will soon be drained. Its eye
That gave all summer, wet blue or wet grey,
Acknowledgement of some sort to the sky

Will hold its socket like a begging bowl
For its own blindness. Dry leaves, runnels of rain
Will crawl across its surface. Not till snow
Spreads its white lint across that concrete plane

Shall I look at its blank concavity
Without regret for summer's liquid lie:
Two feet of water – how it seemed to give
Acknowledgement of some sort to the sky.

Jane Smith

Red October

After summer's cool and wet
Suddenly sunshine, bright and hot,
Late September into a red October.
The beaches filled, the parks crowded up
And life became a time-out holiday
Everyone smiling, friendly, happier -
A little startled by the sudden change.
Whatever winter may bring
We had a break into a red October.

PS Drayson

Fall

Spiking the white air
A last shake-out of yellow stars
On sycamore twigs

Rain sprouts bright lake bangles
Scudding then loosening to loops
Wobbling a bird's path

Moor hen muddles through
Higgledy angled like kale
Choppy lily pads

Afloat in damp cold
Lucid pink September rose
Marks this as our time

Lay us in layers
Of damp lime tree lemon hearts-
Best of leave takings

Tessa Anslow

The Blizzard

All day the snow worked with the wind, so hard
That all the world outside my window frame,
Was lines in Indian ink sketched on a white card;
Hill, mill, meadow and farm without a name.

And on the blurred skyline I looked amazed
At buried churchyard where St Mary's bell
Tolled for the flawless Creation God erased,
And called His own redeemed from whitest hell.

Roger Taylor

Seeing

I looked up and saw
three magpies, flying in line
and right overhead:

What of the saying,
`One for sorrow, two for joy' –
three for ecstasy?

Once, I saw fifteen
Of them, round a clump of bushes,
In a mown field:

How should they be called
In such numbers –
A magnificence of magpies?

Roy Batt

Mates

The peacock opened his gorgeous tail;
flaunting, immodest, dramatic, male;
his colours were dazzling, his aim – display,
to capture a mate; to conquer, to sway.

The peahen stepped modestly in his path,
delicate, timid, a stranger to wrath.
Her bright eyes followed his every move,
an ordinary female looking for love.

She longed for a tail, to sparkle, to win
the energised male, that love could begin.
He saw only himself, the desire to possess;
she was eager for friendship, a glance, a caress.

In spite of this seeming clash of desire,
the two are a pair, and each other admire.

Jean Wallis

Stag Beetles

I halted as they came across my track,
With walk deliberate and mechanical –
One beetle mounted on the other's back.
I thought what moved these things primaeval
Was surely not love; as they staggered,
Armour-shelled, more ox-blood red than black.
Until the smaller female, lighter antlered,
Spread heavy cased wings and took sudden flight,
Leaving her clumsy suitor still aground,
Pincers agape with nothing left to bite;
As if his slow clockwork was now unwound.

Roger Taylor

Bratton

Passed old farm-yard gate
furls slim, muddied vein

a curious crowd pressing faces to fence.

Passed field seared with
stone, bronze, iron and

salt fleshing nubile bodies
swaying to wind:

      pale ballerinas—

the earth at their feet lays pregnant and wild.

      Through the carpal-tunnel
In green who runs the line

of the top of the hill,
where captive spectres play

the sheet of the ground like pin-pricks in skin.

The steady, calf-heavy
crawl through dorsal aorta
beneath mid-evening lowe,
to the beat of muddied feet
on argumentative stone —

arranged like cracked palms of tilled hands.

Across a road, three sore souls
bring day to bear with raise
of a glass or two

before shuddering home.

The staid sound of church bells.

Felix Ortiz

Totleigh Barton

The mornings here are magical
As dawn hits frost-tipped lawn,
Time to slip away, thick booted
Moments alone in damp crisp cool.

We are an ark of thatch and whitewash
Drifting in a sea of rolling hills,
The pheasant's screech accompanies
The sound of pens and wrestling thoughts.

We are creating here, or not,
In the rhythms of the day
Art but also factions,
Connections, notes and lunch.

Yet soon it will be over,
For this disparate band of writers
The life-boats have been sighted,
The shore not far behind.

Rachel Buchanan.

Nether Stowey

Haphazard and plaintive, birds scarp,
Black scraps coughed upwards
From a choking fire.

Yellow bleeds down
Through abcissing trees:
Dead vein spread.

My road lurches on, to the dirty mustard crud
Or a sick throat beach
And the thick grey unconscious beyond.

Tessa Anslow

In Extremadura

High up, in Extremadura, the extremely hard land,
There's a town which said of itself, `Soldiers and priests':
Barracks and seminaries even then abandoned,
But we bought cakes at the convent (was it on Wednesdays?)
On Sundays, people might make a little excursion
To the hermitage above the reservoir.
Over the altar, in a clear glass window,
Our Lady's statue, Guardian of the Gate,
Could be made to revolve, to keep watch over Plasencia.
Outside, cowbells jinked across rough grazing.
Among the boulders, families lit illicit fires
And ate together. I found somewhere apart
And wedged myself among the friendly stones
That felt to me like the walls of an unbuilt house:
Almost a hermitage for almost a hermit.
That was a place. Bleached sky, pale water far below.
My place I call it, though neither belonging nor building.

Jane Smith

Josefov *

Marzipan brickglow, dove soft domes
canopy these corners. They lived here.
Those who squabbled over who'd seen Golem, God.
mooched in coffee houses, set a match
to big-wheeled utopias, rolled them
through visionary fairs, their cigars
burning holes in the edicts, their fist
fast thoughts bouncing off the walls:
bakers, kabbalists, linguists, fabulists,
rabbis, butchers, composers, clerks;
those who elbowed through compacted streets
kissed with salted herring tongues
are names photocopied by guides.

Kafka's face has divorced his skeleton's
untouchable dust. Matinee Idol balloon
drifting onto cafe walls and sugar packets
ghost-synching in the multi-media museum's
deep carpeted black. The phone that barks
cryptic German phrases to thrill the tourists
can't séance him back. Nor can Terezin's
children stop gnawing on their candied
yellow stars, or drawing wire spiral birds
inside the Spanish Synagogue. Green gold
stars implode, reverse across the ceiling,
whisper 'here' 'here' and 'forever'.

*the Jewish Quarter in Prague

Jane Sherberkov

Waiting for Aurora

Inside the Arctic Circle
Clouds started to disperse.
Excitement in the air
Encouraged us to patiently
Look at the diamond sky.
Something obscure was occurring
A vast dark half-moon shape
Haloed with pale light filled the horizon.

Aurora announced her appearance.
Emerald green shards cut through the
Profound blackness,
The shards, now a tiara, dancing awhile
Before melting into candyfloss,
Changing into ribbons, swirling
And mingling with her sparkly audience,
An icy wind pierced my whole being,
I no longer felt human,
And just as I thought Aurora would
Freeze me out of existence,
She relented, languished, disappeared,
Her performance was over.

That night I dreamed of my dead daughter.
She was singing to me
With a voice like crystals
And with the gaze of an angel.
She had love in her eyes
Then, like Aurora she faded away
And I woke up.
Aurora Borealis was real, Jo did have a life
Both are a memory.

Rywa Weinberg

Olvera, Andaluçia 2012

I see the sunlit moon, magical, through the
bare black branches of a winter tree. You
always in my mind, beautiful and lucid.

I look yet again at the painting you gave
me. It is alight with your inner light, deep
yet sunlit colourings – an intense yellow, green.

There is something more; is it joy, boundless?
Joy at the golden rich orderly harvest from
The black-dark, rain-filled, storm-troubled earth?

There are over a hundred strong, nourishing stooks.
The shaded greens of trees and bushes curving
freely around the hill-top, where blue buildings stand.

It is light, joy, colour caught in a numinous whole.
I am changed as I wonder at your explicit mastery –
An enchanted scene, capturing life and hope.

Anthea Bennett

Land Without Maps

This is a land without maps
  where only the sun charts the sand.
Desert birds fly low where clouds
  Appear as pictures upon a camel's back.

This is a dry land where the spirit roams free
  where there is fear in endless undulations
which mystify. No certainties, no comforts
              endless sandscape.

Yet here a sense of eternity echoes
              Some thing of hope.

P S Drayson

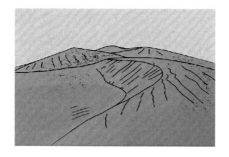

Contributor's notes:

TESSA ANSLOW: lives with her young family In North London, and teaches English to secondary school children.

DAVID ANTHONY BANN: has finished a PhD in Epidemiology at UCL, and tries to balance creative and scientific interests.

ROY BATT: Retired Veterinary surgeon 6 Volumes: most recently (2011) *RETURN TO STRASBOURG*, all Hub Editions. Editor of *MY CONSTANT ENDEAVOUR* an anthology of poems by Veterinary Surgeons and nurses pub 2012.

ANTHEA BENNETT: worked for thirty-five years as a lecturer in history and politics at the London School of Economics. Ist vol. *POEMS OF LOVE AND LIFE OBSERVED* pub. 2008 Lilyville Press.

RACHEL BUCHANAN: new Director of Ludlow Assembly Rooms, an arts venue in rural Shropshire, after ten years living and writing in London. She knits more here.

ARIA DATTA: First breath, Calcutta; Education, London & Accra; Maths read/ researched/taught, London & Dundee; Daughter & Mother in Golders Green, still in wonder finding Nature's phenomena & emotions in an equation or a poem....

PAULINE DRAYSON: lecturer in theatre studies and writes for newspapers and magazines. One vol. *AFTERWORDS* (2008) interested in wildlife, nature studies, music, literature and art. Currently working on a new book of poetry

JOHN JARVIS HANDS: former drama therapist and teacher. 2 vols. *EARTH BOUND, SKY BORNE* (1997) and *SOME TREES and a FEW FLOWERS*, was published by Dragonfire Press October (2008).

LESLEY HANNAH: aka Lesley G Lyndel lives in an off-white ivory tower close to Hampstead Heath. Her first vol, Gods in Recovery, is a work in progress

HANNAH KELLY: 9 vols. Selected Poems pub. 2011: Lilyville Press.
Meritorious Citation. Services to Literature. Oblate at Tyburn Convent.

JUDETH MILLER:(Group Chair) Hypnotherapist, counsellor, trainer. One Vol: *A LONG MALACHITE VIEW* published by Lilyville Press. 2008. Recently pub: RSC website, Adelaide Road project; Postcards from Leather Lane; N2 Anthology:.

FELIX ORTIZ: Currently studying English Language and Literature at The Open University. these poems are a sample from a larger body of currently unpublished work.

JANE SHERBERKOV: lives and works in her native London. She has had poems published in Magma, the Barnet Prizewinner's Anthology and Postcards From Leather Lane. She also writes plays and comedy.

RACHEL SILBERT: Has been writing poetry since arriving in London in 1979.
7 vols. Walking Softly published most recently.

JANE SMITH: Previously published in Camden Poetry anthologies as Jane Hoopell.

ROGER TAYLOR: Retired railways travel officer and community carer. Christian lay-preacher. Now living in Shropshire.

JEAN WALLIS: Has retired from her working life as a librarian mainly in Camden. Enjoys studying Art, Languages and Theatre.   1 vol. *THE TANGLED ROSE* pub. Lilyville Press. Co-editor of N2.

MARJORIE WARDLE: is a retired Music Therapist and still works as an accompanist to singers.

RYWA WEINBERG: retired from administration jobs varying from opera to a psychotherapy clinic. She now enjoys piano practice, music, art, swimming, gardening and dreaming of re-visiting the Arctic.